A Kalmus Classic Edition

Johann Sebastian

BACH

PRELUDES AND FUGUES OF THE WELL-TEMPERED CLAVIER

VOLUME I
Nos. 1-8

Edited by
FERRUCCIO BUSONI

FOR PIANO

K 03096

Introduction.

To the foundations of the edifice of Music, JOHANN SEBASTIAN BACH contributed huge blocks, firmly and unshakably laid one upon the other. And in this same foundation of our present style of composition is to be sought the inception of modern pianoforte-playing. Outsoaring his time by generations, his thoughts and feelings reached proportions for whose expression the means then at command were inadequate. This alone can explain the fact, that the broader arrangement, the "modernizing", of certain of his works (by Liszt, Tausig, and others) does not violate the "Bach style" — indeed, rather seems to bring it to full perfection; — it explains how ventures like that undertaken by Raff, for instance, with the *Chaconne** are possible without degenerating into caricature.

Bach's successors, HAYDN and MOZART, are actually more remote from us, and belong wholly to their period. Rearrangements of any of their works in the sense of the Bach transcriptions just noticed, would be sad blunders. The clavier-compositions of Mozart and Haydn permit in no way of adaptation to our pianoforte-style; to their *entire* conception the original setting is the only fit and appropriate one.

The spirit of Mozart's piano-style is handed down, in a form internally weakened but externally enriched, by HUMMEL. With the latter begins that phase of musical history which deserves to be termed "feminine", wherein Bach's influence, and consequently his connection with the composing virtuosi of the pianoforte, grows weaker and weaker — parallel with the comprehension of these gentlemen for Bach's music.

The unhappy leaning towards "elegant sentimentality", then spreading wider and wider (with ramifications into our own time), reaches its climax in Field, Henselt, Thalberg and Chopin**, attaining, by its peculiar brilliancy of style and tone, to almost independent importance in the history of pianoforte-literature.

But with BEETHOVEN, on the other hand, new points of contact with the Master of Eisenach were evoked, bringing the advance of music nearer and ever nearer to the latter; nearest of all in Liszt and Wagner***, the characteristics in the style of either pointing directly Bach-ward, and completing the circle which he began. The attainments of modern *pianoforte-making,* and our command of their wide resources, at length render it possible for us to give full and perfect expression to Bach's undoubted intentions.

It therefore seemed to me the proper course to pursue, to begin with a digression from the "Well-tempered Clavichord" — a work of so high importance for the pianoforte and of such comprehensive musical value —, that I might trace and show (from the very trunk, as it were) the manifold outbranchings of modern pianoforte-technic.

Although we owe to CARL CZERNY — a man whose importance is derivable in no small measure from the fact, that he forms the intermediate link between Beethoven and Liszt — the resurrection, so to speak, of the "Well-tempered Clavichord", this admirable pedagogue handed us the work in a garb cut too much after the fashion of his period; hence, neither his conception nor his method of notation can pass unchallenged at the present time. BÜLOW and TAUSIG, advancing on the path opened by the revelations of their master,

---

* This piece, originally written by Bach for solo violin, was arranged by Raff for full orchestra.

** Chopin's puissant inspiration, however, forced its way through the slough of enervating, melodious phrase-writing and the dazzling euphony of mere virtuose sleight-of-hand, to the height of teeming individuality. In harmonic insight he makes a long stride toward the mighty Sebastian.

Mendelssohn's "Hummelized" piano-style, overflowing with smoothly specious counterpoint, has naught in common with Bach's rock-stirring polyphony, all earlier and persistent arguments to the contrary notwithstanding. On the other hand, Mendelssohn's successful efforts to inaugurate performances of Bach's works, must be set down as redounding to his credit.

*** The truth of this assertion, as regards Liszt, shows most clearly in his magnificent *Variations* a *motive from Bach* ("Weinen, Klagen"), and in the *Fantasia and Fugue on B, A, C, H.*

Conversely, the *recitatives* in Bach's Passions stand nearest, among all classico-musical productions, to Wagner's spirit, both in respect to their expressional form and depth of feeling. [Comp. Note 3 to Prelude VI.]

Liszt, by his interpretations of the classics, were the first to attain to fully satisfactory results in the editing of Bach's works. This is abundantly proved, in particular, by Bülow's masterly edition of the *Chromatic Fantasia and Fugue,* and Tausig's *Selection* from these Preludes and Fugues.

Much will be met with, in the course of this work, which substantially agrees with Tausig; but identical passages are rare. In this connection I beg to quote from a letter written by the poet Grabbe to Immermann concerning a proposed translation of Shakespeare: "Where I could use Schlegel", he writes, "I did so; for it is ridiculous, stupid, or vain in a translator to leap aside over hedges and ditches, where his predecessor has made a path for him".

The need of an edition as complete* and correct in form as possible has induced the editor, in this attempt to furnish such an one, to bestow upon his work the most painstaking and conscientious attention, reinforced by more than ten years' study of this particular subject. The present edition, however, also aims in a certain sense at re-founding, as it were, this inexhaustible material into an advanced method, on broad lines, of pianoforte-playing; this aim will, however, be carried out principally in Part. I, that being preponderant in the variety of its technical motives.**

The present work is also intended as a connecting link between the editor's earlier edition (publ. by Breitkopf and Härtel) of Bach's *Inventions,* forming on the one hand a **preparatory school,** and his concert-editions of Bach's *Organ-fugues* in *D* and *E♭,* and of the *Violin-Chaconne,* which will serve, on the other hand, as a **close** to the course herein proposed.

Following these last, the study of further *pianoforte-arrangements of Bach's organ-works* is recommended, namely:

> Liszt, *Six Preludes and Fugues.*
> — *Fantasia and Fugue, G*-minor.
> Tausig, *Toccata and Fugue,* D-minor.
> d'Albert, *Passacaglia.*

When these works have been thoroughly learned, both musically and technically, every really ambitious student of the piano ought to take up the still unarranged organ-compositions of Bach, and try reading them *at sight* with as great completeness and richness of harmony as is possible on the pianoforte (doubling the pedal-part in octaves wherever feasible). The manner in which this is to be executed, is suggested in the *Examples of Transcription* given as an Appendix to Part I.

Still, this comprehensive course of study in Bach's piano-music forms but a *part* of that which is necessary to make a thorough pianist of a person naturally gifted. If this truth were stated in plain terms by every conscientious teacher to zealous beginners, the standard wherewith people are now-a-days content to compare the artistic and moral capacities of students would speedily be raised to a height inconveniently beyond the reach of the generality. By such means a barrier might gradually be built up against dilettantism and mediocrity, and thus against the degeneration of art, — a barrier which might cause many to pause and reflect, more carefully than present conditions render needful, before risking a leap and a possible breaking of their necks.

---

* Tausig unfortunately left the *greater half* of the work untouched, several keys being unrepresented in his Collection; even the monumental *B♭*-minor fugue in Part II (to mention one instance) is omitted; neither can he escape the censure of having reproduced certain incorrect readings of the Czerny text. — Bischoff's and Kroll's praiseworthy efforts were confined for the most part to a critical textual revision. Recent good editions are those by Franz and Dresel, Louis Köhler, Jadassohn, Reinecke and Riemann. The chief aim of this last revision is analytical phrasing and anatomization. Analyses in book-form have also been published by Riemann and still earlier by van Bruyck.

** The editor does not for a moment imagine that he is able to exhaustively accomplish this task alone. He will be well satisfied if he should succeed in disclosing a broader horizon for the study of Bach's works, and in formulating a plan for successfully bridging over the interval between the "Well-tempered Clavichord" and modern piano-technic.

New York, January, 1894.

Ferruccio B. Busoni.

"The Well-tempered Clavichord"

by

JOHANN SEBASTIAN BACH.

Revised, annotated, and provided with parallel exercises and accompanying directions for the study of modern pianoforte-technic

by

FERRUCCIO B. BUSONI.

Prelude I.

Moderato.

Part I.

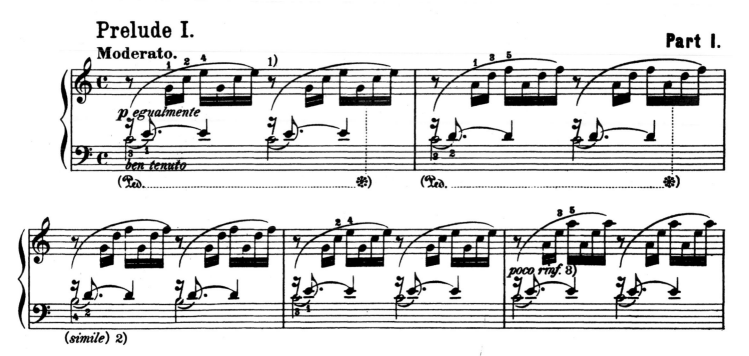

(simile) 2)

1) The flowing and even movement in sixteenths must be kept up between the 8th and 9th notes in each measure, and between the successive measures; do not play: 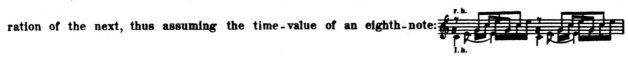 or thus(!):

2) The Editor recommends abstention from the use of the pedal up to the 5th measure of the 3d section, and the strict holding-down of the left-hand notes instead, which very nearly gives the effect of the pedal.

3) Tausig's conception of this prelude, requiring a p i a n i s s i m o execution throughout, is likewise deserving of notice, and forms an entirely new study.

NB. I. For the attainment of a perfect legato, practice the figure first in a n d a n t i n o tempo, with a somewhat firm touch, and in such a way that each tone in the right hand is successively held down through the true duration of the next, thus assuming the time-value of an eighth-note:

II. Then try to obtain the effect of the original notation by playing the figure thus:

Allegro, *leggiermente.*

right hand.
left hand.

etc.

III. This Prelude is also adapted for the practice of an energetic staccato in the following arrangement. In practicing this staccato, care must be taken to render the interchanging of the hands perfectly smooth and even.

Allegro moderato.

etc.

IV. Finally, this Prelude may also be usefully employed for the study of the lightest staccato (in close imitation of the "springing bow" on the violin). The following arrangement will serve as a preparation for the 4th number of the Liszt-Paganini études.

Allegro vivace, *leggierissimo.*

etc.

tenuto, quasi effetto di pedale.

meno tenuto

p

cresc. - - - -

2) Ped.   Ped.   Ped.   Ped.

più - - - -

Ped.   Ped.   Ped.   Ped.   Ped. ....

(ossia: *fz sempre forte* - - - - - - - - - - - - - - - - -)

fz

Ped. ....   Ped. ....   Ped.

(ossia: *ff.* - - - - - - - - *molto largamente ed armonioso* - - - - - - - *allarg.* - - - - - *ff.*)

p   *dolce*   *p* 4)

Ped.   Ped.   Ped.

4) The Editor desires to caution against an over-valuation, or possible under-valuation, of this piece. To quote from Riemann, it is simply a "portal" to the entire work; forming, however, in its euphony and structural finish, a highly satisfactory musical introduction.

Fuga I, a 4.

Moderato, quasi Andante.

1) The theme is equal in length to 6 quarter-notes, or 1½ measures in 4/4 time. As the parts follow each other in close succession, without intermediate episodes, the entrances at S. and B. produce a shifting of the 4/4 rhythm, resulting in an apparent 3/2 measure.

2) S stands for Soprano, A for Alto, T for Tenor, and B for Bass; they always indicate the entrance of the theme. The notes on the upper staff are for the right hand throughout; those on the lower staff for the left hand only.

3) The 3d and 4th quarters in the bass originally conceived thematically:

4) According to the **formal structure**, the double-bar belongs here; according to the **polyphonic form**, the soprano and bass close half a measure further on.

5) The bass phrase is a mutilation of the theme; here the stretto simply grows freer. In the last measure of the development but one, the tenor alone remains "thematic" — the sole survivor, as it were, of the battle between the parts; in the last measure we even lose every trace of the theme.

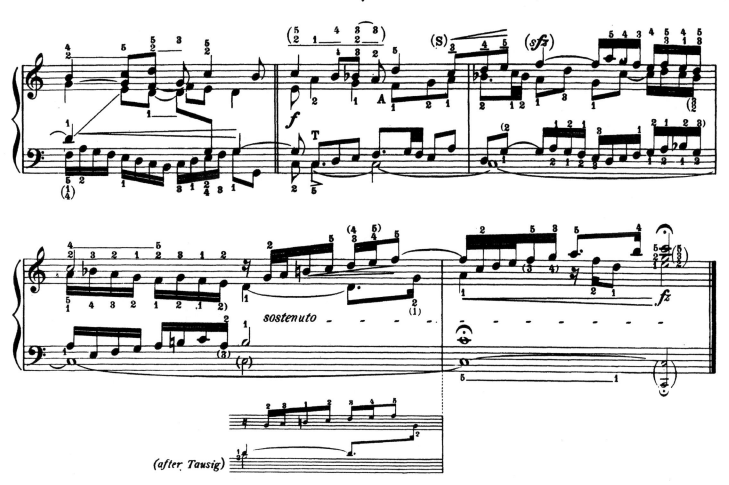

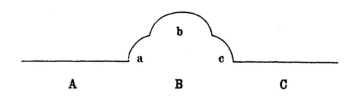

(after Tausig)

NB. A fugue so architectonically perfect in construction as this will be met with, in the course of Part I, in possibly one other case — that of the notable E♭-minor fugue, whose "architectural style" is, to be sure, entirely different. Here the culminating effect is massed in the middle; whereas in the E♭-minor fugue the insatiable upward striving presses onward to the very last measure.

The **exposition** (the successive appearance of the theme in each of the four parts, with alternation between the **tonic** and **dominant** keys) embraces 6 measures, and may be represented graphically by a straight line. The **development** then follows in three sections, the **middle** one being that most replete with contrapuntal devices, while the third development-section gradually leads back into the "straight line" (**Coda**).

Retaining our architectonic comparison, we feel tempted to illustrate the scheme of this fugue by means of the annexed figure:

conformably to which we have

A = Exposition, 6 measures

B = Development, 17 measures
{ a = 7 measures = Stretto
{ b = 5 measures = continually narrowing Stretto (climax)
{ c = 5 measures = simple Stretto again, and return to rest.

C = Coda. 4 measures = Organ-point on the tonic.

Praeludium II.

Allegro con fuoco.

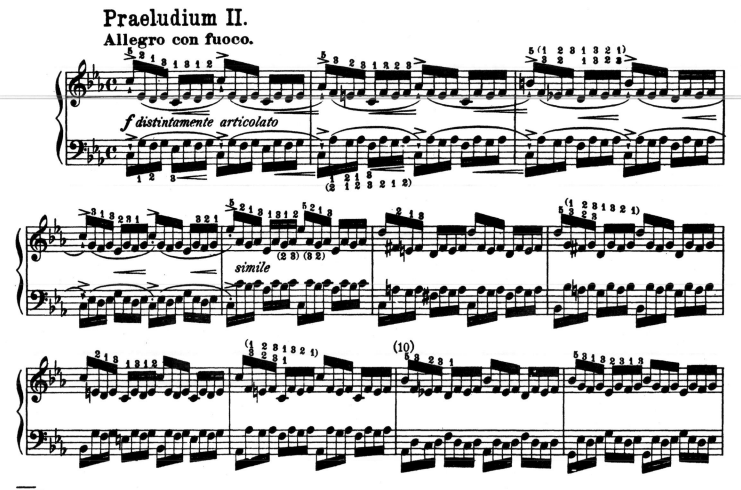

NB. The technical utility of this Prelude—which is comparable to an agitated stream reflecting the flames of a conflagration—may be enhanced: a) by a strict holding of the notes with both little fingers; b) by a martellato variation of the principal figure with an "alternate striking of the hands in double notes" (Zweigriffen); or c) by added octaves, thus rendering the whole a study of sixths in "transcendent execution".— This Prelude (as Bach wrote it) also makes an excellent preparation for the study of the trill with the 1st, 2d, and 3d

fingers, e. g.

Studie. (*Etude.*)

1) In the Editor's opinion, the first period ends with the 14ᵗʰ measure in the relative key, and the second with the next 18 measures, just before the Presto. This latter embraces, together with the Coda, 14 measures more, (reckoning the Adagio as 4 allegro measures); hence the generally satisfactory symmetrical effect. This division, too, best accords with our natural perception.

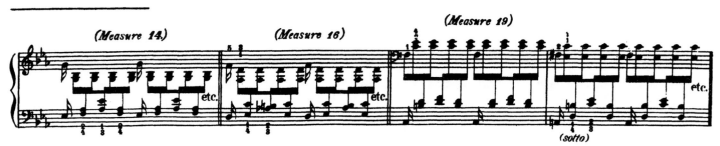

2) The artist must know, among other things, how to husband his strength for climaxes and turning-points, and how to seize opportunities for gathering new strength. This consideration makes the addition of a hold (⌢) over the *G* in the left hand appear justifiable; it should lend to the bass a certain organ-like ponderousness, and throw the Presto—"bearing down all barriers" with its irresistible flood— into yet stronger relief; the point of rest thus gained before this quasi cadenza will also enable the player to recover the necessary lightness and elasticity, which are apt to suffer from 24 measures of an obstinately monotonous movement. Finally, this same left-hand *G* may be transformed, by adding the lower octave and employing the Steinway third pedal (pedale de prolongement, or sustaining-pedal), into an effective 6-measure organ-point.

8) The tempo to be taken here is four times as slow as that of the preceding movement, so that a quarter of the Adagio corresponds to an entire measure of the Presto. Supposing it to be played without a change in time-signature, the following reading would yield a rhythmically correct execution:

The difference between the 32d-notes and 64th-notes is apt to be overlooked by pupils, who thus find themselves entangled in most extraordinary measures: the above simplified notation will aid them in finding the right way. The character of this episode is that of a broad "recitative-style."

Fuga II, a 3.
Allegretto, vivacemente.

1) The counterpoint in eighth-notes to be played staccato throughout.

2) At first sight, one is easily tempted to take the first half of this measure in the Soprano for a continuation of the preceding sequence,—the more so, because the sequence actually goes on in the bass for another half-measure. It is for the player to separate, in the phrasing, the entrance of the theme on the second eighth-note from the episode, and to bring it out by proper stress on the notes.

NB. Its pleasing, almost dance-like rhythm, its subject progressing by the simplest of intervals, and hence easy of apprehension, and its striking economy of contrapuntal devices, have made this fugue, perhaps, the most popular one in the whole collection. Taken as a whole, the development may be regarded as a single long episode (divertimento), which is thrice divided, at regular intervals of time, into shorter sections by the entrance of the theme. So much for the polyphonic form; according to its formal structure, this part consists of twice 8 measures.

3) The two passages to which attention is called are not exactly easy to play correctly,— the counterpoint in a light staccato, the theme in due relief, the syncopation strictly observed. Practice slowly, in this way:

4) The added octaves in the bass were brought into vogue by Czerny. The Editor, however, agrees with Franz and Dresel in allowing them first to enter with the entrance of the theme, and also supports the opinion, that this addition cannot be considered a violation of Bach's style.

Praeludium III.

Veloce e leggiero.

1) This reading is also authentic, and finds logical confirmation in the 2ᵈ measure of the 2ᵈ section:

2) ♪ is later consistently transformed into eighth-notes in the up=beat, thus:

3) The Editor plays this after-struck $g\sharp$ with the clean thumb-stroke from the joint, keeping the wrist quiet but not rigid. The rhythm is marked and supported by the broken-chord figure in the left hand, which must be struck with precision.

4) The 8 eighth-notes of this measure are commonly played in an undefinable species of time, according to which each of them has a time-value of approximately 8 sixteenth-notes. This mistake is inevitable when the sixteenth-note figures in the foregoing 6 measures are conceived as triplets — a weakness to which dilettantes and the like are prone to succumb. The cadence must be played strictly in time and with strong emphasis, sounding, as it were, like a sudden resolve.

Studie. Etude.

Technische Varianten zu Praeludium III.[1)]
Technical Variants of Prelude III.

Da eseguirsi il più fedelmente possibile in tempo e carattere del pezzo originale.

1) This study must not be taken up until the o r i g i n a l, which requires what might be termed a "flying" execution, is fully mastered technically.
A further preliminary exercise is obtained by transposing the latter into *C*-major.

Fuga III, a 3.
Allegro moderato.[1]

At first smoothly and gracefully; then with a gradual intensification.

mp sempre distintamente il ritmo.

Other phrasings of the theme, e.g., *may be equally correct.*

---

1) Riemann's proposed tempo-mark "Andantino piacevole" might easily lead to a certain inappropriate lassitude of movement and expression very prejudicial to this fugue, in which rhythmical culminating-points and strongly marked phrasing are indispensable.

2) Literal execution *the next measure in same way.*

3) Through 3½ measures the key is equivalent (on the piano) to *F*-minor. This idea will facilitate playing them by heart.

4) Here the downward leap of a seventh in the theme is inverted to the upward step of a second.

5) The authentic readings are *b♯* in the left hand and, in the next measure, *g♯* in the right; not ▦ and ▦, the ordinary and incorrect readings.

6) With the last 1½ measures the 2d section ends, they, at the same time, forming the commencement of the 3d section (*M*). Combinations of this sort are not uncommon in polyphonic forms (compare, for instance, No. 11 of Bach's I n v e n t i o n s in the Editor's edition, and also the middle movement of Beethoven's Sonata, Op. 109, in Bülow's edition.)

The subdivisions above proposed, indicating the natural boundaries within the development, will be found to have the satisfactory proportion of 9 : 19 : 9 measures; it is evident, that the middle section is about twice as long as either of the others.

In the Editor's judgment, the third principal division now following is to be regarded simply as an e p i - l o g u e, wherein all that has been said before is repeated in concentrated form, though the true contrapuntal development comes to a standstill. Henceforward, the principal key is, on the whole, adhered to; the brief transient modulations merely serve to establish its domination more and more, whereby the entire conclusion attains to the very height of affirmative energy.

7) Here the theme appears as if interwoven in the figuration of the highest part; modulation from the dominant key to that of the tonic. It is as if the Soprano answered itself in the key of the higher fifth, anticipating any further reply by returning at the same time to the principal key and reaching a definitive close.

These two last measures in the Soprano might be skeletonized as follows:

Praeludium IV.

Andante serioso, non troppo sostenuto ed espressivo.

1) The time is to be imagined as having two beats to the measure ($\flat.\times2$) to prevent a possible dragging of the tempo.

2) The measures between the two NB's are, formally speaking, only a melodic prolongation of the cadence,— an interpolation somewhat in "recitative-style," forming in any event a highly effective deferment, and thus an enhancement, of the final strain. The movement as originally conceived, supposing this "parenthesis" omitted, may be reconstructed as below, plainly showing the internal connection of the measures immediately preceding and following the 1st and 2d NB. respectively:

NB. Through the chaste melancholy of these tones there sounds a note of suppressed pain, bursting forth only at rare intervals,— a Passion-like strain for whose expression a truly devotional mood, and an earnest conception of the full depth and grandeur of Bach's style, can alone suffice. Ingeniously devised nuances will not avail; even mature artistic powers cannot dispense with what is termed, in common parlance, "mood" "inspiration". It follows, that the marks of expression and shading which occur throughout the piece are meant, and can serve, merely as suggestions, and not as absolute directions.

Fuga IV, a 5.

Gravemente e sostenuto, ma non troppo.[1]

1) The eighth-notes of the counter-subject should roll on in a tranquil, stately movement, to which the general tempo must conform.

2) The counter-subject ![notation] plays, in the first section of the exposition, an important (almost obbligato) rôle, which is to be borne in mind in the execution.

3) Wherever a moving part touches, in its course, a t i e d note in another, so that they sound in unison. the note in question is to be struck again, out of regard for the moving part.

4) We willingly assent to Riemann's view, that the next 18½ measures may be considered as a s e c o n d e x p o s i t i o n, albeit one incomplete in fact and effect on account of the omission of the soprano and of the 1st alto. In place of these, however, the 2d alto in this supplementary exposition brings out the theme t w i c e; this 2d alto _ not the 1st, as Riemann asserts _ is to be regarded as the final exponent of the theme.

By the partial notation of the theme on three staves, the Editor hopes to facilitate a comprehension of the contrapuntal scheme.

б) The 3 quarter-notes in the auftakt (up-beat) of the 1st counter-subject are variously modified in the course of the development; the chief variations are etc.

6) From this point up to the Coda, the 1st counter-subject plays an entirely obbligato rôle; i. e., it becomes the persistent and constant companion of the principal theme.

Likewise obbligato up to the very end. Do not make the two staccato quarter-notes too short.

7) Follow out the beautiful leading of the 1st alto, which takes up successively the principal theme, and the 2d and 1st contra-subject. Also follow the bass at beginning of 3d section: here the succession is different.

8) The chromatic imitation between soprano and 1st alto, commencing here and continuing to the end of the second section, should be brought out prominently.

NB. In this fugue we seem to be borne upward, out of the crypt of a mighty cathedral, through the broad nave and onward to the extreme height of the vaulted dome, Midway in our flight, the unadorned gloom of the beginning is supplanted by cheerful ornamentation; mounting to the close, the structure grows in austere sublimity; yet the presence of the unifying idea is felt everywhere,— the single fundamental motive leaves its impress on every part.

Praeludium V.

Allegro con spirito e molto scorrevole (Quasi „alla breve).1)

leggiero, granulato

p

simile

1) The rising and falling of the figuration (in the first section) should be accompanied by a corresponding swell and subsidence in the dynamic shading-nuances, which, being felt rather than audibly expressed, are too ethereal for expression by written signs.

2) In view of the intimate relations between this figural motive and that of the well-known *A*-minor fugue (publ. separately) by the same master the latter— a five-finger exercise par excellence— should be taken up together with this prelude. The left hand taking its full share in the execution of the figure, the following transcription of the prelude, for both hands, will offer few difficulties after the fugue-study is completely mastered.

Allegro vivace.

or thus:

To the "positive" of this perpetuum mobile Chopin's Etude Op. 25, No. 2, und the Finale to his *Bb*-minor Sonata, furnish the comparative and superlative. Of course, this comparison refers chiefly to the technical form. less to the musical content. of these pieces, so different in many respects. But all three are alike in happiness of conception and unity of mood.

Fuga V, a 4.
Allegro moderato ed eroico, piuttosto Andante.[1]

1) The tempo may be approximately determined by stating, that the 32$\underline{d}$ notes of the Fugue are about equal to the sixteenth-notes of the Prelude.

2) Take care not to play the dotted note too long, or the sixteenth-note too short— mistakes to which teachers' ears have long since grown accustomed; not this way  but so When accompanied by the figure in 32$\underline{d}$ notes, the proper execution is sufficiently obvious.

NB. Thanks to its rhythmico-plastic forcefulness and the exceeding simplicity of its contrapuntal construction (note, for instance, the carelessness with which the four-part structure is held together in the 3$\underline{d}$ section), this fugue divides the honors of popularity with its rival, the fugue in C-minor. However, it is none the less a characteristic piece of the first rank, and finds most effective expression in this fugal form.

Besides this, the thematic relations between Prelude and Fugue are closer than may generally be assumed; their common harmonic basis would render it possible to superimpose the one piece on the other, (of course, with some modifications). E. g.

Praeludium VI.
Un poco agitato, non allegro.

1) (The directions under № 1, Prelude V, are also to be observed here.)

2) That is, to be struck somewhat shorter than the treble notes, but not with a dry tone.

NB. This Prelude is to be played *non legato* throughout. In this style of touch the fingers strike the keys elastically without aid from the wrist, and the finger which is down springs back from the key before the next finger falls. This style of touch differs, however, from the true *staccato* in that the tones, although separated one from the other, should have as s o f t and s u s t a i n e d a sound as the nature of the case permits.

A suitable preparatory study to the foregoing is № 10 of the two-part I n v e n t i o n s by Bach (in the Editor's edition); a useful a f t e r - s t u d y is furnished by the Prelude itself, played through several times with-

out using the thumb: etc.

At this stage, the Editor considers it proper to call attention to the importance of the *non legato* touch, as the style in closest sympathy with the n a t u r e of the p i a n o f o r t e. In it is to be sought, for example, the secret of the "pearly" touch, which is based on the same preconditions of separatedness, softness, and evenness. The *legato* touch favored by the earlier school is, in point of fact, non-attainable on the pianoforte, even if _ in isolated instances _ an effect be produced which is illusively like a true legato.

Close acc. to: Friedemann Bach's

The chase after an ideal legato is a relic of that period in which Spohr's violin-method and the Italian art of song held despotic sway over the style of execution. There obtained (and still obtains) among musicians the erroneous notion, that instrumental technic ought to be modelled after the rules of singing, and that it the more nearly approaches perfection, the more closely it copies this model so arbitrarily set up for imitation. But the conditions— the taking breath, the necessary joining or dividing of syllables, words, and sentences, the difference in the registers— on which the art of singing is based, lose greatly in importance even when applied to the violin, and are not in the least binding for the pianoforte. Other laws, however, produce other— c h a r a c t e r i s t i c — effects. These latter, therefore, are to be cherished and developed by preference, in order that the native character of the instrument may make itself duly felt. In proof of the staccato nature of the pianoforte, we instance the enormous development which has come about, within a few decades, in wrist - technics and octave - playing, to receive detailed mention under Fugue X.

By regularly transposing the first note of each triplet into its higher octave, this prelude is transformed into a modern Étude for broken chords in open harmony. In this form, it may (and should) serve as a preparation for the similar larger Études by Chopin and Henselt:

8) This cadence sounds indisputably like a presage of the chromatic runs so characteristic of Liszt's music; even the flower of modern chromatics is rooted in the tone-weft of Bach, as might be proved by numerous examples. This again confirms the remarks in the Introduction.

In conformity with the proposed "transcription" in open harmony, this cadence would sound best in this form:

In the preceding measure (including the tied *g* in the **auftakt**) (up-beat) the original version may be retained.

Fuga VI, a 3.
Andante espressivo.

1) In this Fugue, and those coming after, Ƨ denotes the inversion of the theme in the Soprano (theme in contrary motion), Ʌ= in the Alto, ⅃= in the Tenor, Я= in the Bass.

2) The Bass, in this measure, should be conceived as a transcription (or rather a corruption) of the theme:

3) In each case, the trill belonging to the theme is to be executed as shown in the Exposition.

4) Both of the two 4-measure periods so marked (at the close of the development, 1st section, and the conclusion of the fugue) are perfectly symmetrical as compared one with the other. The second (Tonic) is an exact transposition of the first (Domin.). This method of procedure, so frequently employed by Bach, is important as typical of the sonata-form later evolved.

General View:

I. Exposition = 9 measures (the Bass finishes the period a measure before).
     Episode = 3 measures.

II. Development. {Section 1 = 8 measures (close in dominant key)
               {Section 2 = 8 measures (in 8th measure, alto begins the 3d division)

III. Coda. {Section 1 = 10 measures;
      {Section 2 = 6 measures (the first 4 indentical with the closing measures of Devel., Sec. 1.)

Praeludium VII.

(Introduction.)

Allegro deciso.[1]

1) The tempo-marks, and also the perfectly logical division of this Prelude into an "Introduction" and "Fugue", are to be credited to Riemann, and were taken from his analysis of the "Well-tempered Clavichord."

2) In the coming Fugue we shall see this figure in sixteenth-notes utilized as the counter-subject to the theme.

8) According to Kroll and Bischoff, this tied eighth-note is not c^2 but d^2. This idea, however, appears equally contradictory to the scheme observed in the foregoing 4 measures and to our harmonic sense, which hears in this figuration the dominant seventh-chord of $B\flat$-major. Consequently, we write c^2 in the place in question.

4) The theme of the coming Fugue, and also to a certain extent the "skeleton" of its development and stretto, are presented here in advance; this might be compared to a chapter-heading briefly setting forth its contents.

Tempo I [1]
(Fuga a 4)
(C.S.)

non *f*

B

T

5) Here the fugal theme is quite fully presented ![theme] Its rhythmic form, however, has still to undergo a transformation.

6) Kroll and Bischoff let the Tenor enter here on *e♭* (in unison with the Bass). Riemann, instead, erroneously substitutes the A l t o, making it skip down from *e♭* to *a♭*, while the Tenor breaks off entirely. In reality, the Alto does not take up the theme till the 6th measure; at first, from its position, apparently taking the place of the Tenor part, it resumes in the next-following measure the place in which it naturally belongs. The Soprano does not participate in the Exposition of the theme.

The following notation seems more conformable to the leading of the parts:

8) In order to bring out the culminating point more prominently, the Editor suggests that a doubling of the Bass part in octaves appears not inappropriate. According to this view, the left-hand part would stand thus:

Fuga VII,[1] a 4.
Tempo giusto.

1) The more sportive Fugue originally inserted here seems utterly incongruous to the Prelude, so boldly out-lined in conception and structure. Riemann's remarks confirm this opinion. Contrariwise, the $E\flat$ major Fugue in Part II exhibits, both in its theme and in the broad, vigorous working-out, a striking kinship, an "elective affinity", to the foregoing Prelude,— giving birth to the fancy that we have, as it were, to do with a supernumerary development-section of the "Fugal Prelude" (omitting the ornamental counter-subject). The liberty which the Editor has taken in setting this fugue in the place of the legitimate incumbent, is justified by the circumstance, that Bach was apparently influenced, in his arrangement of the series, solely by the order of the keys. If the two volumes had originally been issued together (there was an interval of 20 years between!) it is quite likely that Bach would have partly interchanged their contents, pairing several preludes and fugues in a manner different from the present. In any event, the graceful, not very weighty $E\flat$-major Prelude in Part II, stands in a more sympathetic relation to the first $E\flat$-major Fugue than to the second.

A comparison of the themes in question is calculated to support the editor's opinion.

It will also be of interest to note, that the subject of the g r e a t *Eb*-major (triple) F u g u e f o r t h e o r g a n must likewise be considered as belonging to this same family of themes. This subject reads:

Prelude (from Part I.)

Fugue (from Part II.)

in Division I:
and in Division III
even:

(rhythmically identical with our Prelude.)

An obbligato counter-subject in sixteenth-notes, developed in Division III of the Organ-Fugue, completes the resemblance of the latter with the Prelude now under consideration.

We are, therefore, fully justified in the conception, that these 3 *Eb*-major fugues form (intellectually) one work, or at least 3 workings-out of one and the same idea as 3 branches from one parent stem, a conception wherein Bach's inexhaustibility is presented to our renewed astonishment.

As mentioned in the Introduction, an arrangement of this triple organ-fugue is embraced in the course of study mapped out by the Editor.

2) We here meet with a rare example. The second section of the executory part shows a p o i n t o f r e s t. This becomes the more conspicuous and effective owing to the contrapunctal development being resumed with full energy in the tenor part.

8) The following transcription, which allows of doubling the Bass part in octaves, is offered as setting forth in fullest vigor the characteristic ponderousness and sturdiness of this Fugue.

Praeludium VIII.
Lento.

1) The right foot should hold the pedal down for the time marked by the h o r i z o n t a l line, releasing and depressing it as marked by the vertical and oblique lines.

Suggestions for the execution:

8) The e^2b in the Soprano ought fairly to "sing"; give the middle part expression, but less prominence.

9) The soft pedal need not be retaken till the entrance of the "misterioso", 3 measures further on.

NB. This deeply emotional movement, emanating from the inspiration of a devout dreamer, is Bach's prophetic forecast that in the fullness of time a Chopin would arise. Whoever is able to look beyond the external form, or to penetrate into the depths, will admit the mysterious affinities subsisting between this Prelude and Chopin's Étude Op. 25, № 7.

The execution of long-breathed melodies on the pianoforte is not only difficult, but positively u n n a t u r a l. In no case can a tone be evenly sustained, and a swell is still less possible; yet these are two indispensable conditions for the rendering of c a n t a b i l e passages, and impossible of fulfilment on the piano. The connection of one sustained tone with a following tone is perfect to a certain extent only when the second tone is struck with a softness precisely corresponding to the n a t u r a l decrease in t o n e of the first. While the tone of the pianoforte, by reason of the instrument's mechanism, naturally increases in power and sonorousness in the d e s c e n d i n g s c a l e, the melody requires, on the other hand, that intensifications, as a general rule, shall be accompanied by an increase of tone-power when a s c e n d i n g;— but beyond a certain pitch the duration of the piano-tone becomes so short, that pauses and breaks in the melodic continuity are absolutely unavoidable. It is the function of the t o u c h, to overcome these difficulties and to counteract these defects as far as may be. To avoid plagiarization of various remarks made by Thalberg on this point, I quote literally a few passages from the Preface to his "L'Art du Chant appliqué au Piano". This course appears to be the best, in view of the fact that these remarks are noteworthy, and yet already forgotten.

<<1) One of the first requisites for the acquisition of a sonorous style of playing, and a tone at once full and adaptable to all nuances, consists in the attainment of perfect freedom from rigidity. It is, therefore, indispensable to possess, in the forearm, wrist, and fingers, the eminent suppleness and versatile flexibility that characterize the voice of a skilful singer. (See Note on pag. 35.)

2) In broad, chaste, dramatic melodies very much must be exacted from the instrument and as full a tone as possible drawn from it; yet this ought never to be sought by striking the keys hard, but by taking them with a short stroke and p r e s s i n g t h e m d o w n deep with a warm, powerful, energetic touch. For simple, tender melodies the keyboard should be k n e a d e d, as it were, with a boneless hand and fingers of velvet; in this case the keys must be f e l t o f rather than s t r u c k.

5) Always avoid in playing that ridiculous and tasteless mannerism in which the melody-notes are struck at an exaggerated interval of time after their accompaniment, so that from beginning to end of the piece the impression of a continuous succession of syncopations is produced.... We urgently advise that the notes be sustained, giving to each its f u l l t i m e - v a l u e. To this end, especially in playing polyphonic compositions, a change of fingers on keys already held down must be diligently looked to. In this connection, we cannot too highly recommend to youthful artists the slow and conscientious study of the Fugue, as the sole method of training the hand for the proper mastery of the polyphonic style.... The p e r f o r m a n c e of a simple 8 or 4-part Fugue, and its correct and appropriate interpretation in moderato tempo, requires and gives proof of more talent than the execution of the most brilliant, swift, and intricate pianoforte-movement.>>

The infinite diversity in the minute shadings of the tones, which is at the command of the best-equipped modern pianist, is not applicable, however, in its full extent to the interpretation of Bach's "concert-pieces". The successive shades should follow each other in a more a b r u p t and unprepared fashion, like changes in registration; in most cases, too, the same shade of expression should extend unvaried throughout an entire movement.

The method of marking the (indispensable) pedal which we have adopted for this piece is n o t absolutely binding, but will serve as a p o i n t d'appui for individual applications.

Fuga VIII,[1] a 3.

Andante pensieroso, non troppo accentato.

1) Stated briefly, this Fugue is the most important in the Book— perhaps in the whole First Part. This is mentioned in order that the player may be aware, from the very start, of the full moment of the task to which he addresses himself.

2) According to the Editor's analysis, there are three sections within the Development which form divid-ing-lines; of these, that in the middle is nearly as long as the two others combined. Thus, the propor-tions are similar here to those in the development-section of the C♯-major Fugue (the third in this book.) The general analysis follows:

Development { I = 10½ measures _ Stretto in similar motion.
II = 22 measures _ Developm. and Stretto in contrary motion.
III = 10 measures _ Stretto in both the above varieties.

The third division of the fugue contains an effective intensification of what goes before; the augmentation of the theme is here added to all the devices employed up to this point, entwined in an intricate contrapuntal maze; the trouble of following out these combinations will be richly repaid. _
Special attention should be paid to the masterly construction of the Fugue.

8) The leading of the two highest parts, which frequently cross, comes out more clearly in the notation given below. The Soprano (theme) should be emphasized.

4) **S, A, T, B** denote theme in the Soprano (Alto, Tenor, Bass) in augmentation, (i. e. the time-values of the notes are doubled). The appearance of the theme in augmentation is indicated, furthermore, by a horizontal bracket ⌒.